THE END OF APARTHEID

BY JASON GLASER

Gareth Stevens
PUBLISHING

Please visit our website, www.garethstevens.com. For a free color catalog of all our high-quality books, call toll free 1-800-542-2595 or fax 1-877-542-2596.

Library of Congress Cataloging-in-Publication Data

Names: Glaser, Jason, author.
Title: The end of apartheid / Jason Glaser.
Description: New York : Gareth Stevens Publishing, 2019. | Series: History
   just before you were born | Includes index.
Identifiers: LCCN 2018020796| ISBN 9781538230268 (library bound) | ISBN
   9781538231395 (pbk.) | ISBN 9781538233191 (6 pack)
Subjects: LCSH: Apartheid--South Africa--Juvenile literature. | Race
   discrimination--South Africa--Juvenile literature. | Blacks--South
   Africa--Social conditions--Juvenile literature. | South Africa--Politics
   and government--Juvenile literature. | South Africa--Race
   relations--Juvenile literature. | South Africa--History--Juvenile
   literature.
Classification: LCC DT1757 .G57 2019 | DDC 305.800968--dc23
LC record available at https://lccn.loc.gov/2018020796

First Edition

Published in 2019 by
Gareth Stevens Publishing
111 East 14th Street, Suite 349
New York, NY 10003

Designer: Sarah Liddell
Editor: Therese Shea

Photo credits: Cover, pp. 1, 25 Louise Gubb/Contributor/Corbis Historical/Getty Images; newspaper text background used throughout EddieCloud/Shutterstock.com; newspaper shape used throughout AVS-Images/Shutterstock.com; newspaper texture used throughout Here/Shutterstock.com; halftone texture used throughout xpixel/Shutterstock.com; p. 5 Jeff Schear/Stringer/Getty Images Entertainment/Getty Images; p. 7 (inset) TUBS/ Wikimedia Commons; pp. 7 (main), 19 Htonl/Wikimedia Commons; p. 9 Anrie/ Wikimedia Commons; p. 11 Print Collector/Contributor/Hulton Fine Art Collection/ Getty Images; p. 13 UniversalImagesGroup/Contributor/Universal Images Group/ Getty Images; pp. 15, 17 (main) Bettmann/Contributor/Bettmann/Getty Images; p. 17 (inset) HelenOnline/Wikimedia Commons; p. 21 STF/Staff/AFP/Getty Images; p. 23 AFP/Stringer/AFP/Getty Images; p. 27 (main) MIKE PERSSON/Staff/AFP/ Getty Images; p. 27 (inset) File Upload Bot (Magnus Manske)/Wikimedia Commons.

Printed in the United States of America

CPSIA compliance information: Batch #CW19GS: For further information contact Gareth Stevens, New York, New York at 1-800-542-2595.

CONTENTS

Words in the glossary appear in **bold** type the first time they are used in the text.

BORN A CRIME

South African comedian Trevor Noah describes himself as being "born a crime." That's because his parents broke the law by even having him. When Noah was born in 1984, it was illegal for black women and white men (and white women and black men) to have children together. Even being seen together put Noah's family at risk of being punished.

Apartheid ruled South Africa when Trevor Noah was young. Apartheid gave power to white citizens while keeping those who weren't white poor and **oppressed**. It kept people divided: white from black, **culture** from culture, and even men from women. Apartheid wasn't one law or a set of laws. Instead, it was a policy that guided the creation of laws. It affected all parts of life.

MORE TO THE STORY

The word "apartheid" means "apartness" in Afrikaans, a language spoken in South Africa. In the United States and Canada, it's often pronounced: ah-PAHR-tyt. However, some people say it differently depending on where they're from.

AS A COMEDIAN AND HOST OF THE TV SHOW *THE DAILY SHOW*, TREVOR NOAH USES HUMOR TO DRAW ATTENTION TO IMPORTANT ISSUES AROUND THE WORLD.

THE IMMORALITY ACT

In South Africa, it was illegal for white people to date or marry black or mixed-race people under the Immorality Act of 1927. This was meant to keep races separate. If blacks and whites were found out to be together romantically, it could mean jail time for the black person but usually a warning for the white person. If the couple had a child, the government could put the child in another home or an orphanage.

THE FIRST SOUTH AFRICANS

Inequality in South Africa began with the land itself. Although South Africa is large—about as large as the state of Alaska—only parts of it are good for farming. Early Africans living in those areas learned how to grow crops and raise cattle. Where growing crops or keeping livestock wasn't possible, people gathered plants to eat or hunted animals. A few communities balanced their needs with both hunting and farming.

Peoples in southern Africa grew into many distantly related but culturally different communities. White traders and settlers who arrived later saw all Africans as belonging to one of only three groups rather than the many rich cultures they actually were. In the settlers' minds, the Africans were hunter-gatherers, farmers, or a mix of both, and they often used offensive labels to refer to each.

MORE TO THE STORY

Traveling by sea near southern Africa wasn't easy. Bad weather, rough waters, and dangerous rocks along the path wrecked many ships.

TRADE BRINGS EUROPEANS

Europeans and African peoples began coexisting in what became South Africa in the seventeenth century. European trading ships bound for India started taking a route around the southern tip of Africa. Traders had learned that farmers on the Cape Peninsula had food, animals, and fresh water. Since trade voyages were months or even years long, this was an ideal area to dock for supplies and repairs.

TABLE BAY

CAPE TOWN

SOUTH AFRICA

CAPE PENINSULA

CAPE OF GOOD HOPE

NORTH AMERICA

EUROPE

ASIA

AFRICA

SOUTH AMERICA

SOUTH AFRICA

AUSTRALIA

ANTARCTICA

FALSE CLAIMS THAT MUCH OF SOUTHERN AFRICA WAS "UNINHABITED" WAS A WAY FOR EUROPEANS TO JUSTIFY TAKING LAND FROM NATIVES.

THE DUTCH ARRIVE

In 1647, a group of Dutch traders were forced to stay in South Africa for a winter after their ship was wrecked in a storm. The time they spent there convinced them it would be possible to create a settlement in the area. The Dutch established the first European colony in South Africa near Table Bay in 1652. That settlement, Cape Town, is the capital of South Africa today.

The Dutch soon spread beyond the settlement. A handful of traders claimed sections of farmland to grow crops to supply arriving ships. Over time, more Dutch settlers and French exiles called Huguenots traveled to South Africa. By the end of the 1700s, colonists controlled the west and were increasingly pushing native peoples out of other regions.

MORE TO THE STORY

Dutch settlers **infected** native Africans with deadly illnesses such as smallpox. The Khoikhoi who lived closest to the colonists were nearly wiped out in the 1700s. One report said fewer than 10 percent survived.

THIS PAINTING, CREATED IN THE 1800S, SHOWS DUTCH
OFFICIAL JAN VAN RIEBEECK (CENTER IN BROWN HAT)
ARRIVING IN TABLE BAY IN 1652. THE AFRICAN PEOPLE
CALLED THE KHOIKHOI GREET THE DUTCH TRAVELERS.

SLAVERY COMES TO SOUTH AFRICA

In 1658, the Dutch began using slave labor in South Africa. Even as they
drove black Africans out, they brought slaves into the country from East
Africa and parts of Asia. Just over a half-century later, there would be more
slaves than colonists. Unequal laws emerged that favored white people
over both free and enslaved Africans. These laws allowed a small number
of white settlers to maintain control over the land.

ENTER ENGLAND

In 1795, British ships seized what was now called the Cape Colony and took control of South Africa and the Asian shipping lanes. Taking over, however, meant constant clashes with both the Dutch and native Africans. The Dutch farmers, known then as Boers, moved into new areas, in part to remain out of reach of British control.

Native Africans, such as hunter-gatherers called the San and the farming Xhosa peoples, continued to lose their homes and lands. Some tried to resettle in remote, less desirable places. Others gave up and worked whatever jobs they could for the British and the Boers for any wage. Dutch and British conflicts increased, and black Africans often had no choice but to join a side.

MORE TO THE STORY

The Boers didn't like living under British laws, which included restrictions on the slave trade and the eventual abolition of slavery itself.

BEGINNING AROUND 1835, LARGE NUMBERS OF DUTCH BOERS BEGAN A DECADES-LONG TREK, OR JOURNEY, NORTH AND EAST IN SEARCH OF NEW HOMES AWAY FROM BRITISH CONTROL. THIS PAINTING OF THEIR "GREAT TREK" WAS CREATED AROUND 1908.

WEALTH UNDERGROUND

At first, European colonists were interested in South African land that could support communities. Settlers took good farmland and basic resources such as water. Once it became clear there was wealth underground, other areas became desirable. In the late 1860s, sizeable diamonds were found near rivers. In the 1880s, treasure hunters discovered veins of gold. Mining both diamonds and gold depended on a large supply of low-wage workers. Native South Africans were often forced into these jobs.

11

WAR IN SOUTH AFRICA

With the British and the Dutch Boers competing for land, war was inevitable—and the blacks of South Africa suffered the most. When war broke out in 1899, the British employed a "scorched earth" policy. They burned homes and farms everywhere they went, destroying the food and shelter of their enemies and native peoples.

Many Boers commanded their black servants to carry weapons, drive wagons, and perform other military duties. Some native groups, including the Tswana people, were forced to aid the Boers, too. Refusal meant fines, punishments, or even prison.

Thousands of blacks, as well as Indians and mixed-race South Africans, joined the British army. Many joined just for food and money. Others joined because they believed a British victory would mean more rights. This belief turned out to be false.

MORE TO THE STORY

The wars fought in South Africa in the late 1800s are sometimes known as the Anglo-Boer Wars, but many scholars call them the South African Wars because all South Africans were affected.

DURING THE WAR, ANYONE THE BRITISH CAPTURED—INCLUDING WOMEN, CHILDREN, AND BLACKS—WAS SENT TO CAMPS AND OFTEN FORCED TO WORK. MORE THAN 14,000 PEOPLE DIED IN CAMPS FOR BLACK AFRICANS, AND NEARLY 28,000 DIED IN THE WHITE CAMPS.

WHO ARE THE AFRIKANERS?

The Dutch Boers became known as Afrikaners, a word which means "Africans" in Dutch. Afrikaners aren't just descendants of the Dutch, though. South African colonists who came from other Western European countries, especially Germany and France, called themselves Afrikaners, too. Over time, Afrikaners developed the language of Afrikaans and a whole culture separate from their European ancestors. Today, about 3 million people in South Africa consider themselves to be Afrikaners. Many still speak Afrikaans.

SEGREGATED SOCIETY

After a peace treaty in 1902, England unified four British and Boer colonies to form the Union of South Africa in 1910. The British and Boers agreed on a common goal: maintaining power over black Africans. The new government set up a system of **segregation**.

For example, the 1911 Mines and Works Act prevented blacks from having many kinds of skilled jobs, reserving those for white workers. The Natives Land Act of 1913 permitted blacks to own only about 7 percent of all land suitable for farming. White people, who were never more than 20 percent of the population, got about 90 percent of the land. This act also created "reserves" for blacks. These areas were the only places black South Africans could buy land.

MORE TO THE STORY

With the Representation of Natives Act of 1936, the few blacks allowed to vote alongside whites in South Africa had this right taken away. Instead, blacks had a different election process in which they voted for a small number of white people to represent them.

LAWS, INCLUDING THE MINES AND WORKS ACT, WERE SET UP TO FORCE BLACK SOUTH AFRICANS TO TAKE LOW-PAYING JOBS, SUCH AS IN GOLD MINES.

SEGREGATED CITIES

Physical separation was also planned between whites and blacks in South Africa. The Native (Urban Areas) Act of 1923 prevented blacks from settling in cities, only permitting them to be there when necessary, such as for work. As a result, rural areas became overcrowded with few job opportunities. However, the government demanded taxes, so families often split up in order to earn money to pay them. Men left their wives and children to travel long distances to work.

APARTHEID BEGINS

In 1948, South Africa held a general election. The Afrikaner-led National Party won the election and committed itself to laws that separated races. This was the official beginning of apartheid.

The Population Registration Act of 1950 **classified** South Africans according to their race. Race was defined by physical appearance, such as skin color and kind of hair, as well as language, where the person lived, and even the friends a person had. The act required people to be identified from birth as white, native (later **Bantu**), colored, or other. Other groupings, such as Indian, were added later.

Under the Natives Act of 1952, black Africans were required to carry "pass books." A pass book included a photograph as well as information about the carrier's place of origin, employer, taxes, and police records.

MORE TO THE STORY

The Reservation of Separate Amenities Act of 1953 made it legal to segregate public places and services according to race.

EXPLANATION OF IDENTITY NUMBER

The identity number consisting of 13 digits and appearing on page 1 of the identity document is made up as follows: (a) The first six digits represent the date of birth of the holder, the first two indicating the year, the next two the month, and the fifth and sixth the day of birth. (b) The following group (four digits) is a serial number and indicates the sex of the person concerned. If the 7th to 10th digits are 0001 to 4999 the holder is a female person, and if they are above 5000 a male person is indicated. (c) The third group of digits (the 11th and 12th) indicates the person's citizenship and population group as follows:

Population group	S.A. Citizen	Non-S.A. Citizen
(i) White	00	10
(ii) Cape Coloured	01	11
(iii) Malay	02	12
(iv) Griqua	03	13
(v) Chinese	04	14
(vi) Indian	05	15
(vii) Other Asian	06	16
(viii) Other Coloured	07	17

(d) The last digit (the 13th) is a control digit forming part of the number.

Kyk bladsy 9 vir Afrikaanse teks.

PASS BOOK

IDENTITY NUMBERS WERE GIVEN TO ALL SOUTH AFRICANS UNDER APARTHEID, BUT ONLY BLACKS WERE FORCED TO CARRY PASS BOOKS WHEREVER THEY WENT.

DEFINING RACE

The way apartheid defined the races in South Africa was completely unscientific. One test involved sticking a pencil in a person's hair. If it didn't fall out, the person was listed as "black." A South African could be reclassified, for example from black to colored or colored to white, which could result in a change of social status. Chinese people were considered "colored," while Japanese people were given "white" status.

Under apartheid, the lands that had been set aside as reserves for blacks were given the name Bantustans. Certain **ethnicities** were assigned to certain Bantustans. For example, if a black South African was of Zulu origin, she was forced to live in KwaZulu, the Bantustan for Zulu peoples—even if she had lived somewhere else her whole life. While government officials promised the residents of the Bantustans independence, they actually stripped blacks of South African citizenship and the few rights and opportunities they had. Blacks still had no choice but to travel to white areas to earn a living for low wages.

The Bantustans were an effective way of keeping blacks of different ethnicities separate from each other as well as separate from a "white South Africa." They prevented blacks from joining together to fight against the government.

MORE TO THE STORY

Black South Africans constructed houses out of whatever materials they could find, including iron, cardboard, and wood.

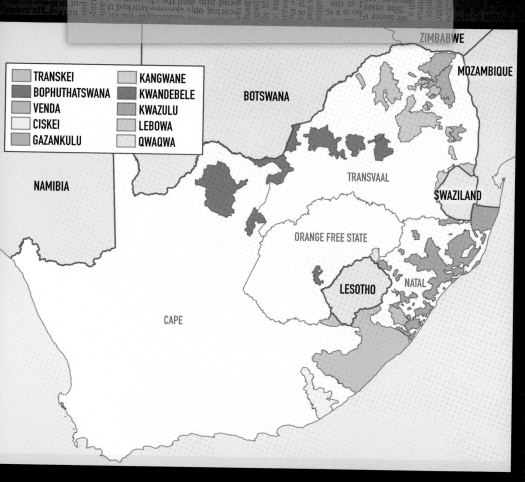

THIS MAP SHOWS THE BANTUSTANS AS THEY WERE
DURING APARTHEID IN SOUTH AFRICA. BANTUSTANS
WERE ALSO CALLED HOMELANDS.

ILLEGAL COMMUNITIES

World War II (1939–1945) brought some change to South Africa. Factories
sprang up to support the war effort, and blacks became the majority
workers in new industries. Black South Africans created settlements near
cities in order to work in these places. They developed their own trade,
political organizations, and labor unions. The creation of the Bantustans
was one way the government fought back against the flood of black
workers to white cities.

THE DEFIANCE CAMPAIGN

Leaders of the anti-apartheid groups the African National Congress (ANC) and the South African Indian Congress organized a movement in 1952 that became known as the **Defiance Campaign**. They encouraged people to take nonviolent action against apartheid through acts of **civil disobedience**, such as sitting on whites-only benches, walking into areas where nonwhites weren't allowed, and using whites-only entrances. Participants sang songs and shouted "Afrika!" to encourage each other.

The government responded by arresting those who took part, most notably a young ANC leader named Nelson Mandela. Protestors usually didn't stay in jail for long because the crimes were considered minor. However, as the protests spread, the government became more concerned. More than 8,000 people were arrested by the end of 1952.

MORE TO THE STORY

Under the Bantu Education Act of 1953, schools taught black South African children how to be unskilled workers and little else. The author of the act, Hendrik Verwoerd, stated: "There is no place for [the African] in the European community above the level of certain forms of labour."

FUTURE SOUTH AFRICAN PRESIDENT NELSON MANDELA FAMOUSLY BURNED HIS PASS BOOK TO PROTEST APARTHEID DURING THE DEFIANCE CAMPAIGN, AS DID THOUSANDS OF OTHERS.

THE AFRICAN NATIONAL CONGRESS

The African National Congress was formed in 1912 by blacks and mixed-race Africans who wished to keep their voting rights. In the 1940s, with an increase in segregation laws, several young leaders changed the ANC's focus to fighting apartheid. The ANC's membership grew. Eventually, the South African government banned the ANC. Some, including Nelson Mandela, later joined the ANC's **militant** group Umkhonto we Sizwe, or "Spear of the Nation."

STATES OF EMERGENCY

The South African government responded to periods of unrest by declaring a "state of emergency." During these times, officials cracked down on apartheid protestors by jailing or exiling them and banning certain activities. During the 1960s, that included banning black-led political organizations such as the African National Congress.

On March 21, 1960, in the town of Sharpeville, police opened fire on protestors demonstrating against pass books, killing 69 people and injuring 180 more, including children. The Sharpeville **Massacre**, as it was called, created outrage around the world where a growing number of people with televisions in their homes could see what was happening.

In 1961, the Union of South Africa became the Republic of South Africa. It separated itself and its apartheid policies from England and the rest of the world.

MORE TO THE STORY

Although people labeled "colored" and "Indian" had representatives in the South African government under apartheid, the representatives of the white population could never be outvoted.

SOWETO YOUTH UPRISING

To protest the Bantu Education Act and the segregated system of education, student movements such as the Black Consciousness Movement and the South African Students Organization rose up to challenge apartheid and were met with force from the police. On June 16, 1976, police opened fire on student protestors in Soweto, southwest of Johannesburg. An angry uprising the next day led to more deaths by police gunfire. One student leader, Steve Biko, was later tortured and killed by police.

IN LESS THAN 2 MONTHS OF UNREST IN 1960, THE SOUTH AFRICAN GOVERNMENT JAILED OVER 18,000 PEOPLE.

POWER TO THE PEOPLE

Even though South Africa became an independent nation, the cruelty of apartheid couldn't be kept hidden from the world. In the 1980s, through **sanctions**, other nations began to put great pressure on South Africa to change. Companies and banks refused to do business there, too. The economic and political pressure became too much. The president at the time, P. W. Botha, was forced to step down.

On February 2, 1990, the newly elected president, F. W. de Klerk, made a stunning announcement: The ban on the African National Congress and other exiled organizations would be lifted, and political prisoners, including Nelson Mandela, would be released. South Africans were astonished, and the responses ranged from joy to anger. In allowing black leaders to operate freely, de Klerk was opening the door for blacks to decide their country's future.

MORE TO THE STORY

Because of international sanctions, the South African government ended a few apartheid laws in the 1980s. However, life for blacks and other people who suffered under apartheid remained much the same until 1990.

F. W. DE KLERK (LEFT) SHAKES HANDS WITH NELSON
MANDELA, FOLLOWING MANDELA'S RELEASE FROM PRISON.
AS THE LEADERS OF THE NATIONAL PARTY AND THE
AFRICAN NATIONAL CONGRESS, THEY WORKED TOGETHER
TO TEAR DOWN APARTHEID.

NELSON MANDELA

Perhaps the most famous face of the apartheid period was Nelson Mandela.
Mandela was a lawyer who organized protests against apartheid. At first, he
followed the nonviolent example of Mohandas Gandhi's protests in India. After
the Sharpeville Massacre, Mandela believed more violent forms of resistance
were justified. The government barred him from speaking in public and
eventually jailed him. Despite being imprisoned from 1962 to 1990, Mandela
remained an important leader of the African National Congress.

REPRESENTATION AT LAST

Publicly, de Klerk's government moved toward a representational government by sharing power with black leaders such as Mandela. Behind the scenes, however, some pro-apartheid forces used violence to stop the process. Even within oppressed groups, the chance for power caused rivals to attack one another. Still, the country pressed on toward an open election, the first in which all South Africans had an opportunity to vote. Nelson Mandela's fame and popularity made him the easy choice for the African National Congress's leader.

Over 4 days in April 1994, more than 19 million people voted. The African National Congress won nearly 63 percent of the vote. Mandela became South Africa's first black president. For the first time, the government was made up of a nonwhite majority.

MORE TO THE STORY

South Africa adopted a new set of laws to govern the nation in 1996. The Constitution of the Republic of South Africa was written by representatives of all major political parties and includes a Bill of Rights banning segregation.

MAMPHELA RAMPHELE

THIS PHOTO SHOWS BLACK SOUTH AFRICANS STANDING IN LONG LINES TO CAST THEIR VOTE IN 1994. EACH APRIL 27, SOUTH AFRICANS CELEBRATE FREEDOM DAY TO REMEMBER THIS **DEMOCRATIC** ELECTION.

WOMEN OF THE RESISTANCE

Many women played roles in combatting apartheid. Founded in the 1950s, the Black Sash was an organization of white women who were supporters of the anti-apartheid movement. Winnie Madikizela-Mandela was as much of an activist as Nelson Mandela, to whom she was married from 1958 until 1996. However, many questioned her sometimes–violent methods. Dr. Mamphela Ramphele was one of the founders of the Black Consciousness Movement. She also created and led the Agang SA political party to fight government corruption.

MORE WORK TO DO

Nelson Mandela and F. W. de Klerk won a Nobel Peace Prize in 1993 for their joint work in peacefully ending apartheid. There are many more wealthy and successful blacks now in South Africa as well as black-owned businesses. Yet the country still wrestles with widespread poverty that affects black South Africans more than other groups, and the anger that has built up over centuries hasn't gone away.

In 2017, whites owned an estimated 72 percent of private land while blacks owned just 4 percent. To correct this overwhelming difference, South African lawmakers voted in 2018 to allow land to be taken away from white citizens without paying them for it. Many wonder if this is fair. Remedying the injustices of apartheid continues to be slow and difficult work.

MORE TO THE STORY

Lack of health care for nonwhites during apartheid allowed the spread of HIV, the virus that causes a disease of the immune system called AIDS. More than 18 percent of adults in South Africa were reported to have HIV in 2016, more than in any other country.

IS IT APARTHEID?

Cultures around the world sometimes struggle with sharing a community. People disagree whether Palestinian people living in Israel, the Gaza Strip, and the West Bank are experiencing a form of apartheid. Some consider the laws regarding how women in Saudi Arabia must behave to be another form of apartheid. Remembering South Africa's apartheid may help prevent injustice elsewhere in the world.

THE RISE AND FALL OF APARTHEID

- **1652:** DUTCH TRADERS CREATE A SETTLEMENT IN CAPE TOWN. EUROPEANS BEGIN TO PUSH NATIVE AFRICANS OUT OF THE TERRITORY.
- **1658:** THE FIRST SLAVES ARRIVE IN SOUTH AFRICA.
- **1795:** ENGLAND TAKES CONTROL OF THE CAPE COLONY.
- **1835:** THE GREAT TREK BEGINS. DUTCH FARMERS SEIZE NATIVE LANDS.
- **1910:** THE UNION OF SOUTH AFRICA IS ESTABLISHED, AND SEGREGATION LAWS BEGIN TO BE PASSED.
- **1948:** THE AFRIKANER-LED NATIONAL PARTY COMES TO POWER, AND APARTHEID IS ESTABLISHED.
- **1950:** THE POPULATION REGISTRATION ACT CLASSIFIES SOUTH AFRICANS ACCORDING TO THEIR RACE.
- **1952:** THE DEFIANCE CAMPAIGN BEGINS.
- **1959:** THE PROMOTION OF BANTU SELF-GOVERNMENT ACT FORCES BLACKS INTO BANTUSTANS.
- **1960:** THE SHARPEVILLE MASSACRE OCCURS.
- **1962:** NELSON MANDELA IS IMPRISONED.
- **1976:** POLICE OPEN FIRE ON STUDENT PROTESTORS IN SOWETO.
- **1990:** NELSON MANDELA AND OTHER POLITICAL PRISONERS ARE RELEASED, MARKING AN END TO APARTHEID POLICIES.
- **1993:** MANDELA AND F. W. DE KLERK WIN THE NOBEL PEACE PRIZE FOR THEIR WORK UNDOING APARTHEID.
- **1994:** MANDELA BECOMES THE FIRST BLACK PRESIDENT OF SOUTH AFRICA.
- **1996:** SOUTH AFRICA ADOPTS A NEW CONSTITUTION, GUARANTEEING EQUAL RIGHTS TO ALL CITIZENS.

GLOSSARY

Bantu: a term describing peoples of South Africa who speak a group of languages spoken in central and southern Africa. It became a label Europeans used for all native peoples and is now considered to be insulting except when relating to language.

civil disobedience: the breaking of a law as a form of nonviolent protest to force change

classify: to assign something or someone to a category or class based on shared qualities

culture: the beliefs and ways of life of a group of people

defiance: a refusal to obey something or someone

democratic: describing a form of government in which all citizens participate

ethnicity: relating to races or large groups of people who have the same culture

infect: to spread something harmful inside the body

massacre: the killing of a large number of people, especially when they cannot defend themselves

militant: having or showing a desire or willingness to use strong, extreme, and sometimes forceful methods to achieve something

oppressed: treated in a cruel or unfair way

sanction: an action that is taken to force a country to obey international laws by limiting or stopping trade with that country, by not allowing economic aid for that country, or by another action

segregation: the forced separation of races or classes

FOR MORE INFORMATION

BOOKS

Erskine, Kathryn. *Mama Africa! How Miriam Makeba Spread Hope with Her Song.* New York, NY: Farrar, Straus and Giroux, 2017.

Mathabane, Mark. *Kaffir Boy: The True Story of a Black Youth's Coming of Age in Apartheid South Africa.* New York, NY: Simon & Schuster, 1998.

Pollack, Pam, and Meg Belviso. *Who Was Nelson Mandela?* New York, NY: Grosset & Dunlap, 2016.

WEBSITES

Apartheid
www.our-africa.org/south-africa/apartheid
Learn about the effects of apartheid through the conversations of South African children and teens.

Apartheid Museum
www.apartheidmuseum.org
Discover much more about the apartheid era on this museum's site.

Civil Rights: Apartheid
www.ducksters.com/history/civil_rights/apartheid.php
Read more facts and see a map of segregated South Africa.

INDEX